T0130037

THE SECRET PLACE
TO HIDE FROM DEATH

DR. ELCO VALLIER

THE SECRET PLACE TO HIDE FROM DEATH

iUniverse books may be ordered through booksellers or by contacting:

iUniverse
1663 Liberty Drive
Bloomington, IN 47403
www.iuniverse.com
1-800-Authors (1-800-288-4677)

ISBN: 978-1-5320-8634-2 (sc)
ISBN: 978-1-5320-8635-9 (e)

Library of Congress Control Number: 2019917187

Print information available on the last page.

iUniverse rev. date: 10/23/2019

Contents

Acknowledgments

No book is a product of one person's work. I have to admit that it took a team effort to make this project a reality. There were times when I felt like I would never get it done. But with the help of God and the encouragement of my family and friends, I finally completed it. First I want to acknowledge God and thank him so much for giving me the will and desire to minister and teach his words. Without you, my Lord and Savior, I would not have been able to accomplish this project. That is why I am dedicating this book to you first, my Lord, and you can make your way with it in the lives of all those who will have a copy in their hands.

I also want to thank my lovely wife, Jacqueline, and our children, Shemaiah, Christina, and Elshamah, for their patience and understanding during my time spent focused on this project. This book is for you, and it is also your achievement. Congratulations!

To all the staff members who helped me from a distance at iUniverse to complete this project, I want to say thank you. You are amazing people, and I could not have asked for a better experience than to be working with you through this journey. Thank you.

Now to all members of the Theophile organization in the United States and around the world, thank you. I would like to express a special thank-you to all my colleagues, who knew about this project and encouraged me to complete it. A special thank-you to the youth, friends, and family. Thank you to Mrs. Denis, Mrs. Alexander, and Dr. Bold. Finally, I want to express my gratitude to all the members of my family, my cousin Mika, and others. Special thanks to my mom, who never stops praying for me and believing in me. Thank you, thank you, and thank you.

Preface

As a pastor, I have had the privilege of preaching sermons on many different topics and ministering to people during their most difficult moments, and I find that one of the most difficult topics to minister about is the death of a loved one. Many times I have reached a point where I really did not know what to say, especially since each of those moments is unique. For me, one of the hardest things in ministry is trying to comfort a grieving family and help them make sense of the loss of a loved one.

The reality of the grieving process hit me when I had to minister to a particular family in my congregation. This family of three—father, mother, and son—modeled the behavior of a loving family. Like most involved parents, the father was making plans for the day and looking forward to picking up his son from school. On that particular day, however, all of his plans came to nothing, because death knocked at his door and took him away from his family while he was sleeping.

Upon notification of this tragedy, I rushed to the family's residence. When I arrived, the deceased body was still in the house, and I remember how the family's plans changed that day. Someone else had to pick up the boy from school, and his mother was inconsolable, not knowing what she was going to tell her son. When the boy learned the news upon his arrival at home, I could see the loss and wonder in his eyes. As his pastor, I asked myself, *What can I say to this child that will make sense to him now?* Could I utter the words *It will be all right*? What Bible verses could I use to show that God still loved him? In his innocent mind, he was just trying to figure out what had happened. In moments like that, I become speechless.

These daunting questions have propelled me to embark on a search for key answers that could help alleviate the pain for many other families going through that same situation. Throughout my ministerial counseling, those moments never escape my mind. This book is a result of the many sermons that I have preached on the topic, my own research, and the echoing words of grief from wonderful families I've met over the years. However, my goal is not to console those who are grieving, for only God can do that, but rather to offer some hope that we can hide from death.

How do we get to the root of the death dilemma? What has been done about this worldwide problem to end the epidemic, and where can we actually hide from death? My investigation and findings are solely Bible based, for I believe there is no better place to find answers to a worldly problem than the Bible. That's where we find the origin and cause of our problems, and where we can find the solutions to those problems. My intention is to present to my Christian families, and to everyone else who is grieving or in the grip of death, the fact that there is indeed a secret place to hide from death.

Introduction

In every life situation, we can agree that to find the solution to a problem, we must first find its source. As we embark on this journey to find the secret place to hide from death, we must first know the cause of death. We cannot deny that death is part of our daily life on earth. Many families around the world experience the loss of a loved one, and the question always asked is this: "Why do people have to die?" This is not a difficult question to answer when we know the origin of death. Our goal is to provide the answer to this question and many more questions that are attached to it. Sometimes we do not realize what a big problem death is until we lose a family member or close friend. Imagine with me how the world is experiencing suffering and pain under the power of death through the following statistics.

According to the Central Intelligence Agency's *World Factbook* and other sources, throughout the twentieth century in the developed world, the leading causes of death transitioned from infectious diseases such as influenza, to degenerative diseases such as cancer or diabetes. In 1900, the leading cause of death in the United States was influenza, with 202.2 deaths per 100,000 people, followed by tuberculosis, which is now curable, with 194.4 deaths per 100,000. In mid-twentieth-century America, the leading cause of death was heart disease with an impressive 355.5 deaths per 100,000, followed by cancer at 139.8 deaths per 100,000. Although death rates dropped significantly in the latter part of the twentieth century, the leading killers remain heart disease and cancer. The United States saw 192.9 people per 100,000 die from heart disease in 2010, followed by cancer with 185.9 people per 100,000.

The world population in the twentieth century experienced much death during the two major world wars. World War II saw the twentieth century's largest number of war-related deaths—between forty and seventy-two million. Other predominant wars in the 1900s were World War I with up to sixty-five million deaths, the Russian Revolution with up to 9 million deaths, and the Afghan civil war and Mexican Revolution with up to two million deaths each. Several other major wars took place in the twentieth century, including the Iran-Iraq war, the Soviet War in Afghanistan, the second Sudanese civil war, the Korean War, and the Vietnam War.

It is estimated that car accidents caused the deaths of around sixty million people during the twentieth century, but war, genocide, and holocausts led to many millions of deaths. In the late 1900s, acquired immunodeficiency syndrome (AIDS) had already killed millions, particularly in Africa and Southeast Asia. Cancer also killed millions because of lifestyle factors and pollution generated by industries. This data does not include deaths caused by crime or natural disasters—tsunamis, earthquakes, volcanoes, blizzards, hurricanes, tornadoes, and so on. Obviously death is a major issue, a powerful force that brings a lot of families to their knees in pain.

In light of this indisputable truth, many people have come to realize that there is no safe haven in this world. No matter what we try, living peacefully on this planet is almost impossible, and no one can understand why. Deeply troubled by this conclusive reality, man has launched a quest for a place to hide from death. Does that place really exist in our universe? And if it does, will we ever find it? In this book, we'll go back to the beginning of the history of humankind to find out how we got here. We'll rediscover the different layers of man's biggest quest since our existence began on earth, to discover if man will ever find this holy grail, the secret place to hide from death.

The Fall of Man

To understand why death exists, we need to look at the beginning, where death began. The Bible tells us that approximately six thousand years ago, man was walking in perfect harmony with his creator in the most beautiful garden on earth, the garden of Eden. I assume it was a pleasant atmosphere, because God's presence was with man, and that the relationship between God and man was perfect. They talked to each other throughout the day and never went to sleep without saying good night. It was the most perfect relationship that humankind has ever experienced.

There were no problems, because man was innocent and had not yet known evil—until the day when everything changed. Man committed a disobedient act that violated God's word, and God decided to judge man accordingly. What was that disobedience? Man ate from the tree of the knowledge of good and evil, from which God had commanded him not to eat. It is written that God said, "You may surely eat of every tree of the garden, but of the tree of the knowledge of good and evil you shall not eat, for in the day that you eat of it you shall surely die" (Genesis 2:16–17). This is where it all began, and God's punishment for man's disobedient behavior was a death penalty.

It is interesting to ask, "Why such a harsh judgment for what seems to be a simple disobedience?" First, we must admit that maybe disobedience in God's sight is a serious sin. Second, we must also admit that maybe God values his relationship with man a lot. God chose this punishment from among all other possibilities, and it sent a clear message that God will not tolerate sin. It must also have been that only death can separate God and man.

That's why the only punishment that satisfactorily solves the problem of a broken relationship with God, from God's point of view, is death. "For the wages of sin is death, but the free gift of God is eternal life in Christ Jesus our Lord" (Romans 6:23). On the other hand, it's also true that death seems to be the only way for man to reconcile with God

(Romans 5:10). We can conclude with the paradox that only death can both separate man from God and reconcile man with God. The next question is "What type of death separates man from God?"

After man ate from the tree of the knowledge of good and evil, he did not die, so what happened? Should we consider death as being only physical, or are there other types of death? We know that God's word is law (Psalm 19), so the fact that Adam and Eve remained alive after they ate from the tree of the knowledge of good and evil means that we should investigate death in its various dimensions. To do that, we must first look at the creation of man to see if anything might have kept him from physically dying as soon as he ate from the forbidden tree.

Genesis 2:7 says, "Then the Lord God formed the man of dust from the ground and breathed into his nostrils the breath of life, and the man became a living creature." In this verse, God tells us how man is composed. We can see the tripartite formation of man in the text: (a) God formed him of dust from the ground, (b) God breathed into his nostrils the breath of life, and (c) man became a living creature. In other words, man is made of dust (body) and the breath of life (spirit), and the result is a living creature (soul, emotions, will, and mind).

The "living creature" reference here presents the idea of mobility, abundant living, joy, wealth, good health, peace, completeness, and so on. To live in less than abundance is not living but surviving. Abundance is not contained in the things that we possess for the betterment of our physical lives, but instead is contained in a rich relationship with God our creator in our spiritual lives. To have physical abundance but be spiritually destitute is simply tragic. Jesus said, "I came that they may have life and have it abundantly" (John 10:10b). "For what does it profit a man to gain the whole world and forfeit his soul?" (Mark 8:36).

Since we can see there are three parts in man's formation, we can conclude that God did not refer only to physical death, but also to spiritual death. Since man continued to walk around after he ate the forbidden fruit, we can conclude that his death sentence was spiritual rather than physical, at least for that moment. In that sense, spiritual death can be defined as God separating himself from man and withdrawing his fellowship, relationship, peace, and friendship. A *soulish* death, in contrast, can be defined as man's change of heart, emotions, and attraction to the things of God or God himself. Remember that the first emotion expressed by man when he heard the sound of God's voice after his sin was "I was afraid" (Genesis 3:10b). Peace was one of the things man shared with God before disobeying Him, but afterward, man became

God's enemy (Romans 5:10, Colossians 1:21). Now fear has replaced peace, sorrow has replaced joy, and the list goes on.

So man's physical death does not separate him from God, but instead it's man's spiritual and soulish death that causes that separation. But what happens when someone dies physically and yet retains a spiritual connection with God? We'll answer that question later, as we continue in this journey to find the secret place to hide from death.

On what basis can we say that Adam's death was spiritual? Let's go back and take a look at what happened next. There's an old saying that "Like attracts like." Let's see if we can apply it in this story since this is, in fact, a spiritual law. The Bible says, "The Spirit himself bears witness with our spirit that we are children of God" (Romans 8:16). This law is different from the electrostatics law that says "Like repels like." Genesis 3:8 says, "And they [Adam and Eve] heard the sound of the Lord God walking in the garden in the cool of the day, and the man and his wife hid themselves from the presence of the Lord God among the trees of the garden."

Adam and Eve hid themselves from God, a sign that they had become spiritually repulsive or unresponsive to God. The spiritual attracts the spiritual, and the carnal attracts the carnal. If man had not died spiritually, he wouldn't have had any reason to hide from God, who is spiritual. Man would have been drawn to God instead of hiding from him. "God is spirit," says John 4:24.

It's also important to note that after man disobeyed God, it was God seeking and calling for man, not man seeking God. Genesis 3:9 says, "But the Lord God called to the man and said to him, 'Where are you?'" Today we have a generation that is not seeking after God, and the only reason for that is sin. Sins put us in the position of hiding and make us unresponsive to God's voice. What a tragedy is sin. So we see now that death has both physical and spiritual dimensions, and that Adam and Eve were spiritually separated from God while they were still alive.

Where Are You?

This question "Where are you?" (Genesis 3:9) is not to be taken lightly, for it is far more a spiritual question than a natural one. After all, what was dead was in the spiritual and not yet in the physical. It was the fellowship, friendship, peace, grace, favor, protection, and eternal that were lost. No one can actually hide from God in the physical or the natural. The psalmist put it this way:

> Such knowledge is too wonderful for me; it is high; I cannot attain it. Where shall I go from your Spirit? Or where shall I flee from your presence? If I ascend to heaven, you are there; if I make my bed in Sheol, you are there. If I

take the wings of the morning, and dwell in the uttermost parts of the sea; even there your hand shall lead me, and your right hand shall hold me. If I say, Surely the darkness shall cover me, and the light about me be night, even the darkness is not dark to you. (Psalm 139:6–11)

The psalmist understood that the Lord God is omnipresent, which means God is everywhere. When God asked Adam, "Where are you?" the question was more spiritual than natural. It is like God was asking, "How far from me have you gone, Adam, in our relationship?"

Let us now hear what Adam had to say. Genesis 3:10 says, "And [Adam] said, 'I heard the sound of you in the garden, and I was afraid.'" Why was Adam afraid? "[B]ecause I was naked." And then Adam did what? "[A]nd I hid myself." God's voice made Adam afraid to the point that he had to hide, but was it supposed to be like that? Remember, God and man had been in perfect harmony, so God's voice should have brought joy, not fear. Unfortunately, that is the result when we let a third party destroy our peace and harmony with God. We suffer a lot of pain. Our cry today regarding death could be because our relationship with God is broken.

Usually people don't hide from their friends, but from their enemies. It's true that someone might be ashamed and hide because of nakedness, but not necessarily because they were afraid of the voice of a friend. Adam wasn't afraid because of God, but because of his own awareness that he was naked. When people victimize other people, they're not afraid of the victim, but of the consequences of their own actions. Adam hid from God because he was naked, so we should investigate his nakedness in the spiritual sense, although it can also be examined in the physical sense.

It is wise to say this has never been about the physical only, but also the spiritual. Apostle Paul put it this way: "For we do not wrestle against flesh and blood [the physical], but against the rulers, against the authorities, against the cosmic powers over this present darkness, against the spiritual forces of evil in the heavenly places [the spiritual]" (Ephesians 6:12). Everything that occurs in the physical also occurs in the spiritual, and vice versa. When Adam said, "I was naked," he may have been indicating that he was stripped of his spiritual protection. We can almost hear Adam saying, "I am now vulnerable, exposed, and unprotected. I have been stripped of my fellowship, friendship, spirituality, grace, favor, peace, companionship, authority, dominion, and Lord God." In other words, Adam was saying that he had lost everything.

It's interesting that Adam did not say, "I am naked and I hear your voice, so I hide myself." Instead he said, "I was naked," using past tense, which means that when the Lord God called him, Adam had already created clothing to wear. Genesis 3:7 says, "Then the eyes of both were opened, and they knew that they were naked. And they sewed fig leaves together and made themselves loincloths." Man had already covered himself before the Lord God called for him. Also, apparently Adam did not feel proud to approach God with his new clothing.

Adam and Eve's nakedness was not primarily a physical problem but a spiritual one. Why? Because their physical clothing did not fully cover them. Adam was still naked, despite the aprons he made to cover his body. He said, "I heard the sound of you in the garden, and I was afraid, because I was naked, and I hid myself" (Genesis 3:10). To be clothed and pleasing to God requires being wholly clothed. Apostle Paul said, "Now may the God of peace himself sanctify you completely, and may your whole spirit and soul and body be kept blameless at the coming of our Lord Jesus Christ" (1 Thessalonians 5:23). Adam was trying to deal with his physical nakedness as the Lord God came into the garden and called him, but Adam's problem was far bigger than that.

The spirit and soul of man needed to be dealt with more than his physical nakedness. Similarly, today we hear an outcry about how the younger generation finds nothing wrong with exposing private parts of their bodies in public places. Their dress code is perfectly fine, regardless of what other people may think, and you dare not tell them that their attire is not appropriate for public view. In fact, they are untroubled about moral values, decency, or even what others think of them, so why should that be different for Adam? Again, the problem is more spiritual than physical. The deeper the spiritual problem, the less concerned we become about the physical. We have a spiritual problem today—not a physical one. The drugs, sex, murder, indecent exposure, and so on result from a deep spiritual problem. If what was lost of Adam was in part spiritual, what was made by Adam must also be viewed as part spiritual. Could it be that Adam making loincloths to cover his nakedness had spiritual significance? We shall explore this possibility later.

Genesis 3:7 says, "Then the eyes of both were opened, and they knew that they were naked." Were they physically blind? No, for they saw that the fruit was good. Therefore the opening of their eyes must been intellectual and/or spiritual, since it is connected to knowledge and intelligence. As soon as their eyes were opened, they *knew* they were naked. The obvious conclusion is that man left his innocent, ignorant phase of life to step into a new era involving the dispensation of conscience, knowledge, accountability, and self-will.

This new era gave man a sense of self-examination, creativity, responsibility, accountability, and the duty to act. Let's look at the text again:

1. They knew they were naked, demonstrating their awareness of their condition.

2. They sewed fig leaves, fulfilling their sense of duty to act.

3. They made loincloths for themselves, demonstrating their creativity, responsibility, and sense of accountability regarding their new condition.

The first thing man ever made to cover his naked condition was clothing. In other words, man's first invention was a cloak to hide his nudity as soon as he became aware of it. These actions will be investigated in a spiritual context so that we can find out what they imply in the spiritual sense. First we will look at man's clothing, and then God's clothing.

Man's Clothing

When man first acquired knowledge, he used that knowledge to come up with his first invention—clothing to hide his physical and spiritual nakedness. Yet that was a weak invention because of the fig leaves of which it was made. The fig leaves symbolized the seasonal, temporary, ineffective, and generally weak nature of his covering. But God, with a knowledge that surpasses that of man (Isaiah 55:8–9), provided sheepskin (Genesis 3:21) as a better alternative. God knew man's clothing could not sustain him after his sin, because man's disobedience changed the order of everything.

Man forfeited his dominion over all of God's creation to Satan, for we are slave to what we obey or serve. Nature was also affected, no longer providing man the desired atmosphere needed for comfortable living. A fig leaf would not have been sufficient when the temperature and weather changed. The apostle Paul put it this way: "For we know that the whole creation has been groaning together in the pains of childbirth until now" (Romans 8:22). This verse tells the effect of man's sin upon the whole of creation. Man's invention was therefore insufficient and unable to save him from this big mess, but what God has provided is eternal and able to deliver and restore.

What if we were to ask, "Was man-made clothing good enough to spare Adam from judgment for his disobedience? Was it good enough to restore him from his sin?" Our answer would be an emphatic "*No!*" Even today, man still thinks he can hide behind his cloak and everything will be all right, though he is inwardly terrified that his cover might not hold for long. Despite man-made loincloths to cover his physical nakedness, he is still afraid when he hears God's voice, because man's internal, spiritual being has not yet been addressed. So should we still question the effectiveness of man's cover?

If man's invention had reconciled him with God, who had then forgiven him for his disobedience, God would not have needed to make new clothing, right? So what clothing does man prefer? Adam could have kept his man-made clothing and completely disregarded God, or he could have accepted God's new clothes as a sign of restoration and redemption— and then lived out of his fear. If you are grieving, don't choose Adam's man-made clothing, which appears religious but has no relationship with God. Instead, choose God's clothing, which is Christ, and end your grieving.

God's Clothing

As we just discussed, man's clothing represented religious practices to appease God and make man feel better about his new condition. Now let's see what God's clothing symbolized. The animal slaughtered by God to make clothing for man was symbolic, representing the ultimate sacrifice that Christ would make to save man from his sins. But what did the aprons made by man from fig leaves represent? Was there any spiritual symbolism in them? Let's be clear that our goal is not to spiritualize things where there is no biblical argument for it, but instead to help us see the end from the beginning (Isaiah 46:10) and the repetition of man's mistakes until this day.

God gave Adam and Eve clothing made from skin to cover themselves, as a sign of restoration, but God had to sacrifice an animal to get that skin. He sacrificed an animal to cover man's nudity—or *sins*, if you will. That tells us that the only thing that will satisfy God, in the mess that man had created for himself, is a blood sacrifice. Something or someone has to die. "For the wages of sin is death" (Romans 6:23a). In Leviticus 17:11, we read, "For the life of the flesh is in the blood, and I have given it for you on the altar to make atonement for your souls, for it is the blood that makes atonement by the life."

This solution, however, was just a temporary fix. "Indeed, under the law almost everything is purified with blood, and without the shedding of blood there is no forgiveness of sins" (Hebrews 9:22), yet it is people—not animals—who sin. Hebrews 10:4 says, "For it is impossible for the blood of bulls and goats to take away sins." If that is true, the *something* option as a substitute to take away sins has now become ineffective, leaving us with only the *someone* option. A man needed to die to cover another man's sins, so we have a bigger problem than we originally thought. Who would be that man? Not everyone will be willing to give his life for someone else. And even if someone was willing to take on that task, would it be acceptable to God? No, because ever since Adam and Eve sinned, every child has inherited their sinful nature, and it wouldn't work for one sinful person to die for another sinful person. There is only one solution—God must provide a sinless man as the only acceptable sacrifice.

But where would God find a sinless man, since everyone born into Adam and Eve's bloodline is sinful? "The fool says in his heart, 'There is no God.' They are corrupt, doing abominable iniquity; there is none who does good. God looks down from heaven on the children of man to see if there are any who understand, who seek after God. They are all fallen away; together they have become corrupt; there is none who does good, not even one" (Psalm 53:1–3). In view of all that is working against man now, the requirement will not change. The sacrifice must be a perfect man dying for the rest of humankind. He cannot be a different species, such as an angel, alien, or anything outside of man's nature. He has to be fully human and go through the process of being born, growing up, and so on. That has left man depending on God to work a miracle on his behalf, but as far as man is concerned, there is little hope of restoration. Thanks be to God, for it was written, "For nothing will be impossible with God" (Luke 1:37). Amen.

Before I dive into God's way of making this impossibility possible, let's go back to our previous thought about the spiritual significance and symbolism of man's fig leaf. We can see that the sacrifice God made by killing an animal was much more spiritual than literal, implying better clothing for man later. It's also possible that clothing made from leaves was not only physical, but also contained spiritual implications regarding the future. Let's look a bit further at the methodology by which God chooses temporarily to accept sacrifices from man. It was through religious ceremonies or rituals that man presented his sacrifice to God to cover his sins. (See Numbers 15.) The killing of bullocks, goats, heifers, lambs, and so on was the forerunner that God provided to man, which would later lead to the ultimate sacrifice of Christ. Based on the method that God prescribed for man, the first hiding place from death was religious rituals or religions.

Religion: Man's First Hiding Place from Death

"**B**ut of the tree of the knowledge of good and evil you shall not eat, for in the day that you eat of it, you shall surely die" (Genesis 2:17). Throughout man's entire existence, religion has played a major role in his life. According to *Webster's New World Thesaurus,* third edition, religion is "all that centers about human beings' belief in or relationship with a superior being or beings." Could it be that Adam and Eve's clothing of fig tree leaves, similar to God's clothing of animal skin, represented a religious practice by which man believed he could establish a relationship with other gods?

Remember, they made loincloths to cover their nudity *before* God called them. Could that suggest that man will once again make cover for himself before Christ returns to earth? I cannot say, but I know that as it was then, so shall it be again before Christ returns. Will man have already made his own loincloth/religion and be worshipping his own god? Many biblical scriptures support this view, and God told us that man will, in fact, make his own religions and worship his own gods.

In Jeremiah 16:20, the prophet asks this rhetorical question: "Can man make for himself gods?" The answer is yes, but then Jeremiah continues, "Such are not gods!" As far as the sovereign God is concerned, they're just idols. The prophet Hosea said, "They made kings, but not through me. They set up princes, but I knew it not. With their silver and gold they made idols [gods] for their own destruction" (Hosea 8:4).

Man can make gods for himself, but all offerings to a god require belief and a relationship with that god. By definition, that is religion. Therefore, to offer a sacrifice to cover man's sin, man has to first believe in and have a relationship with that specific deity. He cannot just build an altar, place a sacrifice on it, and offer that sacrifice to some random spirit floating in the air. He must have *said* something to the deity that he believes is a superior being, and he must *believe* that the deity will accept his sacrifice and grant him forgiveness or whatever he requested.

Man-made or not, there is a deity or superior being behind all religions, and religious rituals and practices are the means by which man connects to that deity. However, it is man's belief in and relationship with the deity that makes things work. Man can sing, dance, praise, worship, and offer sacrifices and offerings all day long, but if he does not have a relationship with the god he claims, nothing will work. In the case of Adam, he makes something that he doesn't believe in or have an intimate relationship with.

When Paul saw the Athenians worshipping gods they did not know, he said, "Men of Athens, I perceive that in every way you are very religious. For as I passed along and observed the objects of your worship, I found also an altar with this inscription: 'To the unknown god.' What therefore you worship as unknown, this I proclaim to you" (Acts 17:22–23). People have often ignorantly worshipped unknown gods. What is it about God that makes man so desperately want to form a relationship with him and worship him? Well, man's creator was God, and the very first thing man saw after he became a living soul was God. Furthermore, man is not man apart from God breathing into his nostrils the breath of life.

Everything about man is of God, and without God, man can no longer be what he was designed to be.

Man was made to connect with and belong to God, and that's why man is always in search of that relationship, which becomes manifest through worship. Man was made to worship, connect with, and belong to his creator, God. Without God, man experiences an emptiness that cannot be filled by anything else, so God has become man's source of life. Nowhere will man feel comfort and peace apart from his creator. This longing to connect brought man to an expedition that has never ended: the quest for God.

Many people deny that they are on a quest for God, but the reality is that we are all searching for a god. Sometimes we create a god to fill our emptiness and make us feel complete, and no one can honestly say that there is no God, unless the search for God was first his passion. "The fool says in his heart, 'There is no God'" (Psalm 14:1a). I believe this fool searched for God and did not find him, so he or she concluded there is no God. That is the case for many atheists. People often misunderstood what it means to search God, and they search for stuff *from* God instead of connection and relationship *with* God. Unfortunately when they don't find the *stuff* they're looking for, they conclude that God does not exist.

Other times, it is bitterness and hatred for God that push a person to deny God's existence. Perhaps it's the death of a loved one from cancer, despite a person's supplication to God, or the injustice that we see around the world. All these things contribute to a decision to conclude that God does not exist, based on a sense of being betrayed by God. Someone might have a great relationship with God, but when that relationship gets tested, he or she becomes doubtful and questions—or even denies—God's existence. Regardless of the reasons, the fact is that we all are searching for God, whether consciously or subconsciously.

The symbolism of man's futuristic religious ritual was embedded in the man-made loincloth that gave Adam a sense of protection and self-acceptance. Adam did not feel acceptable when he was naked, so he made clothing for himself. When he produced a loincloth made of fig leaves, Adam felt relieved. That is what religion does for us today—it gives us a sense of protection and acceptance, but it never completely eradicates our inner guilt. Only God can do that, but it depends on our relationship with him and our willingness to obey and trust him. Remember, despite Adam's cover, he was still afraid when he heard God's voice.

Being religious is not enough. Adam's shame about his physical nakedness was alleviated, but his spiritual nakedness, guilt, and need persisted. If Adam had been relieved of his spiritual nakedness through religion, he would not have been afraid when he heard God's voice. Instead, he would have proudly come out and met God. Are you a religious person? Be careful that you do not fall under the cloak of religious cover-up. Religion was man's first hiding place from death, but it is incapable of saving him, so man has continued to pursue other hiding places from death.

It is not wrong to be religious, but don't use religion as a cloak to hide. Many people claim to be Christians because they belong to a religious group where they profess their faith, but their religion has nothing to do with Christ. Many of them don't even believe that he is the Savior of the world. Belonging to a religious sect doesn't make you right with God—only your personal relationship with God determines your status within your religious practice. Many religious people are running from God, and like Adam, they use the loincloth of religion to hide. Many others are sincerely seeking him through their religious practices in good faith, and they have a true relationship with God. When tragedy hits, belonging to a religious sect can be a great source of support. We find comfort and a sense of relief, but never peace. To find peace, we must have a personal relationship with the prince of peace, Jesus Christ.

The Quest of Man for the Hiding Place Continues

Let us look at another avenue where man had thought to find a hiding place from death. When the serpent approached the woman, many things happened in a short period of time. Again, let's look closely at that conversation:

> He said to the woman, "Did God actually say, 'You shall not eat of any tree in the garden'?" And the woman said to the serpent, "We may eat of the fruit of the trees in the garden, but God said, 'You shall not eat of the fruit of the tree that is in the midst of the garden, neither shall ye touch it, lest ye die.'" But the serpent said to the woman, "You will not surely die.

For God knows that when you eat of it your eyes will be opened, and you will be like God, knowing good and evil." So when the woman saw that the tree was good for food, and that it was a delight to the eyes, and that the tree was to be desired to make one wise, she took of its fruit and ate, and she also gave some to her husband who was with her, and he ate. (Genesis 3:1–6)

Now let's dissect precept by precept the whole thing.

(1) God's word is questioned. Did God actually say, "You shall not eat of *any* tree of the garden"? Questioning God's word creates doubt and confusion.

(2) God's word is added upon. The woman told the serpent that not only could she not eat fruit from the tree in the middle of the garden, but that if she even *touched* the fruit, she would die. Why would she add that? In her exchange with the serpent, she may have added it to reinforce the seriousness of God's command. Also, given that she probably was not pleased with the command, perhaps she took the opportunity to vent by adding to God's word what God never said.

(3) God's word is challenged and contradicted. The serpent said to the woman, "You will not surely die."

(4) God's word is misinterpreted. "For God knows that when you eat of it your eyes will be opened, and you will be like God."

(5) God's word is disobeyed. "She took of its fruit and ate."

Within this conversation, one thing—more than anything else—tempted them to eat the fruit. When the woman saw that the tree was good for food (desire or lust of the flesh), that it was a delight to the eyes (desire or lust of the eyes), and that it would make a person wise (pride of life), she and her husband ate the fruit. The main cause of disobedience was that they wanted to be wise. In order to be wise, we must have knowledge, for wisdom is the right application of knowledge. The tree is called the tree of the knowledge of good and evil, and without knowledge, wisdom is almost nonexistent. The problem is that knowledge often results in pride, which is enmity with God. "But he gives more grace. Therefore, it says, 'God opposes the proud, but gives grace to the humble'" (James 4:6).

Satan, the ancient serpent, found himself in the garden in the first place because of his pride, which had led him to revolt and try to replace God. (See Isaiah 14 and Ezekiel 28.) In the same manner, the serpent encourages man to become independent, self-sufficient, knowledgeable, self-existing, self-cured, self-governed, and so on—just as God is. In order to do that, man must be clothed with knowledge. Could it be that man's desire to attain knowledge and become wise was his second hiding place from death?

Knowledge: Man's Second Hiding Place from Death

As man's knowledge increases, it is amazing to see that he usually begins to believe more in his knowledge than in God, as if knowledge has replaced God. Today, knowledge has become the outcry of passion and the argument of the prestigious, elite, and most educated of our society. What is it about knowledge that the wise, elite, educated, strong and powerful know, and that the feeble, weak, abandoned, and rejected do not know?

Some people even say that knowledge is God, and others that knowledge is power. Only God can say what the wise, the elite, and the sages know about knowledge that the weak, feeble, and ignorant do not. Still, we can explore for clues that might lead us to certain awareness of man's secret discovery of knowledge and his goals for his acquired knowledge. As man has searched for that safe haven, knowledge has evolved into various forms—esoteric, mystical, scientific, medical, political, and so on.

The most elite and enlightened people have become known as the illuminati, those who have presumably been illuminated with greater understanding of certain domains or in secret knowledge that has not been revealed to the common man. The illuminati have reached or been touched by the light of intelligence, known to them as the *third eye*. But where did man get this knowledge, and who taught him how to attain it? Obviously the hiding place for which man is looking is a way to avoid God's judgment, presence, interference, and dominance in his affairs. Man wants to be his own god, and he refuses to be held accountable to any deity. That is another reason why man hid as soon as he heard God's voice in the garden.

Where did man get his knowledge? The Bible contains many references that identify God as the source of knowledge. For example, Proverbs 2:6 says, "For the Lord gives wisdom; from his mouth come knowledge and understanding." In view of this text, and many others, God has always been seen as the sole author of all knowledge. God is omniscient, which means he knows everything, and no form of knowledge is new to him. On the contrary, man is not omniscient and therefore cannot know everything unless it is taught to him.

Regarding the details of God's conversation with man after the fall, certain points are worth highlighting. First, man acquired awareness of his own condition, which can be characterized as moral or intuitive knowledge. Man knew that he was naked and recognized his vulnerability and weakness.

Man also acquired inventive knowledge, which can be described as intellectual or scientific knowledge of his environment. Man sewed fig leaves together and covered himself. With that inventive knowledge came creativity, but also treachery, deceitfulness, and ignorance of better things. What man didn't acquire was sacrificial knowledge—the knowledge of sacrificing, which would have given man the idea of killing an animal to make clothing for himself, as people have done since then. Who introduced that knowledge? Who was the first to sacrifice or kill? Perhaps Cain, in terms of man killing man, but the notion of killing was first introduced by God. Based on how we have come to understand it today, God's introduction of this knowledge was not evil.

Animal sacrifice was an introduction to what must take place to restore and save man. That sacrifice foreshadowed the ultimate sacrifice of Christ to cover and erase man's shame, nakedness, and sin. Through that sacrifice, God taught us this principle: in order to live, one has to die. That was the message from the beginning, as we read in 1 Corinthians 15. As the first to kill for man, God became the first to die for man: "No one takes it from me, but I lay it down of my own accord" (John 10:18). God himself sacrificed that lamb in the garden to make clothes for man.

We can all agree that after man ate from the tree of the knowledge of good and evil, he received some knowledge, but not all knowledge. At the very least, man could then make decisions on his own without having to wait for God's dictation. Man had passed from the stage of innocence to the stage of accountability and conscience, because with knowledge comes responsibility and accountability. Having acquired knowledge, man began to pursue a life that didn't require him to deal with God, and yet he expected to be fine and not face judgment at the end.

Imagine a scenario where man finds a way to live eternally, without having to wait for the eternal salvation that only Christ offers. How would man live, and how much would that breakthrough cost man? Where would man live without having to worry about the death sentence imposed on him by God? I believe that man's experiments in any field of studies—medical, scientific, or mystical—are looking not only for temporary relief or a short solution, but also for a complete cure and eternal victory.

Today man fights death with the many scientific breakthroughs that help us live longer, but man doesn't want to stop there. Man's vision is not to slow the course of death, but to eradicate it completely. If your heart stops, man can often shock it back to work again with cardiopulmonary resuscitation or an automatic external defibrillator. If your kidney fails, dialysis or a kidney transplant can help you live longer. If your lung fails, a mechanical ventilator can help you breathe again. The list goes on and on.

As man pushes toward his goal of attaining an eternal cure, we benefit from temporary relief from all kinds of pain. We are thankful for man's efforts and appreciate his endeavors to find that safe haven from death—and ultimately to defeat death. However, we know better, for man is working to avoid God's judgment of death. Man's ultimate desire is to acquire greater and better knowledge with which to defeat God. Where would man acquire that knowledge? The answer to that question will lead us to the source.

Man's Source of Knowledge

After God asked Adam where he was and Adam said he was afraid, God asked Adam who had told him that he was naked. Let's stop here and digest what's going on. Why would God ask "Who?" rather than "What?" or "How?" If eating from the tree of the knowledge of good and evil had been sufficient to give Adam this knowledge, God would not have had to ask who told Adam that he was naked. Instead, God's first question would have been, "Adam, did you eat from the tree of the knowledge of good and evil?" That was not the case, however, because God knew that some knowledge had to be taught to man. Despite eating from the forbidden tree, Adam hadn't acquired *all* knowledge, for most of it would have to be passed down to him via other sources—such as the serpent, in this specific case. That is why God's first question was "Who told you that you were naked?" (Genesis 3:11).

Where does that leave us? Man eating of the forbidden tree is reactionary, based on his new knowledge. What was that new knowledge? "The serpent said to the woman, 'You will not surely die ... Your eyes will be opened, and you will be like God" (Genesis 3:4–5). To paraphrase, "There is no such thing as death. Instead you will have a lot of knowledge and be like God." The idea is that if man can be like God, death will have no power over him. So the serpent taught man something new, even though it was a distortion of God's word. The lesson that Satan instilled in man was to become as God so that death would have no power over him. At this point, God had two serious problems on his hands. God knew that to change man, you have to change only his mind, for as he thinks in his heart, so is he. (See Proverbs 23:7.) Man's behavioral change results from his thinking; in other words, the mind elicits the behavior.

God's first problem was the answer to "Who told you?"— the serpent. His second was man's disobedience, found in the second question: "Have you eaten of the tree of which I commanded you not to eat?" (Genesis 3:11). The venom that had been inserted into man's head was far more dangerous than man's rebellious reaction. Man's awareness of his outer nakedness was much less important to God than how man came to know that he was naked. Man's inner condition was reflected and then revealed in his outer condition, which had been caused by knowledge. Man's new source of knowledge was poisonous to him, for knowledge can be as poisonous as a snake when it violates God's commands and principles. His new knowledge rendered man empty and spiritually naked before a holy God. Knowledge is a beautiful thing, but it must remain within God's parameters; otherwise it becomes a curse to any society.

Since God's first question to man after the disobedience was "Who told you that you were naked?" (Genesis 3:11), let's investigate man's new source of knowledge. It is clear that the snake caused man to disobey God, but who is the snake? The text clearly explains that the serpent tempted Eve: "Now the serpent was more crafty than any other beast of the field that the Lord God had made. He said to the woman, 'Did God actually say, "You shall not eat of any tree in the garden?"'" (Genesis 3:1).

We just read how the serpent tempted man, but who is the serpent? The serpent was craftier than any other beast of the field that the Lord God had made. I believe the serpent was a divine being, a member of the divine council of God. He chose to oppose God's plan for humanity by prompting humankind to disobey God, so they would be either killed or removed from Eden—and thus away from the plan of God. It's possible that this divine being possessed a snake with which to tempt Eve. Man's rapport was mainly with God and the animal kingdom over which he had been given dominion. Before the temptation, the Bible doesn't mention that man had any interaction with other spirit beings or angels. There is a valid, logical possibility of a snake possessed by Satan, just as an angel of God made Balaam's donkey speak.

Why did God judge the snake if it was simply a victim or bystander? Why was the law of double reference applied if it was simply a snake? God is just, and his justice extends even to the animal kingdom. I believe the snake was not completely innocent—if one chooses to believe the snake theory, which remains a theological debate among scholars. According to the Bible, God also gave laws to the animal kingdom. Genesis 9:2 says, "And the fear of you and the dread of you shall be upon every beast of the earth and upon every bird of the heaven, upon everything that creeps on the ground and all the fish of the sea. Into your hand they are delivered." Animals were to fear man, according to this text. They were also given a basic sense of moral accountability, and they are accountable for murder. (See Genesis 9:3–6 and Exodus 21:28–36.) But I believe the snake was a divine being, not a member of the animal kingdom, because Satan—not a snake—is the author and architect of man's fall. Whatever the form that divine being had taken, snake or not, he remained the author of man's fall.

In Genesis 3:1, *serpent* is from the Hebrew word *nachash*, which has three meanings. The root of *nachash* is *noon*, *het*, and *sheen*—a noun, verb, and adjective in Hebrew. As a noun, *nachash* means "serpent," but as a verb it means "deceiver" or "diviner," which also fits the story. As an adjective, *nachash* means "bronze" or "the shining one"—in Genesis, *ha nachash* or "the shining one." Luminosity is a characteristic of a divine being, not a person or animal, in the Hebrew Bible and the Ancient Near East texts. This is a divine being, not an animal or a man. Would Eve carry on a conversation with a snake? I don't think so, but she *would* talk to a divine being who would be of interest to her. Adam and Eve lived in the garden of God, so they were quite familiar with divine beings.

So what we have in Genesis 3 is not an animal, but a divine being—a throne room guardian, seraph, serpentine being, a member of the divine council in Eden. And this divine being decided to deceive humanity to get rid of them, to get humans removed from Eden, from God's council and family. Why? The scriptures hint at pride or jealousy. The Pseudepigrapha work titled *Life of Adam and Eve* elaborates on the motive and role of Satan in the fall of humankind. In chapter 16, we read, "And the Lord God was angry with me [Satan] and banished me and my angels from our glory; and on your account [man] we were expelled from our abodes into this world and hurled to the ground. Straight away we were overcome with grief, since we had been robbed of such great glory. And we were grieved when we saw you in such joy and luxury. And with guile I cheated your wife and through her action caused you to be expelled from your joy and luxury, as I have been driven out of my glory."

The divine being Satan was jealous of man, so he devised a plan to make man sin against God so he would be kicked out of the garden of Eden. What a villain and snake! Now we are starting to understand from whom man received his knowledge. In the book of Enoch, we find another account that supports the view that man received knowledge from other divine beings beside God, but how? In Genesis 6:1–2, we read, "When man began to multiply on the face of the land and daughters were born to them, the sons of God saw that the daughters of man were attractive. And they took as their wives any they chose." Unions were taking place between the daughters of man and the sons of God, who are spirit beings or angels of God's divine council.

Enoch's Contribution

First Enoch 7:1–7 provides more details about the possibility of man acquiring knowledge from a different source:

> It happened after the sons of men had multiplied in those days, that daughters were born to them, elegant and beautiful. And when the angels, the sons of heaven, beheld them, they became enamored of them, saying to each other, "Come, let us select for ourselves wives from the progeny of men, and let us beget children." Then their leader Samyaza said to them; "I fear that you may perhaps be indisposed to the performance of this enterprise; And then I alone

shall suffer for so grievous a crime." But they answered him and said; "We all swear; And bind ourselves by mutual execrations, that we will not change our intention, but execute our projected undertaking." Then they swore all together, and all bound themselves by mutual execrations. Their whole number was two hundred, who descended upon Ardis, which is the top of Mount Armon.

Satan and some of the fallen angels planned to mess with the progeny of men. Why? After Adam and Eve's disobedience and sin, God investigated the matter and sentenced each of them accordingly. But regarding the sentence of the serpent, we find the law of double reference, for God addressed the serpent as both a member of the animal kingdom (Genesis 3:14) and as the divine being (Satan) who caused man to sin. When addressing Satan, not the snake, God's verdict was "I will put enmity between you and the woman, and between your offspring and her offspring; he shall bruise your head, and you shall bruise his heel" (Genesis 3:15).

God declared a war between the offspring of woman and that of the serpent. Satan knew that a woman cannot produce offspring without a man's seed, so he came up with a brilliant plan. If he could genetically alter man's seed (DNA), all humankind would be corrupt. Then he wouldn't have to fight with them, nor would they be fit to bruise his head as promised by God. Satan is smart—but our God is smarter. God sent a deluge to destroy all of Satan's genetically corrupt seed. Later God surprised Satan with the virgin birth of his offspring, a baby boy from heaven whose name is Yeshua. This is genius from our strong and mighty God. *Alleluia to the Lamb of God!*

During the time of man's mingling with angels before the deluge, man received much knowledge from those divine beings. According to 1 Enoch 8:1, "Moreover Azazel taught men to make swords, knives, shields, breastplates, the fabrication of mirrors, and the workmanship of bracelets and ornaments, the use of paint, the beautifying of the eyebrows, the use of stones of every valuables and select kind, and of all sorts of dyes, so that the world became altered." These things taught to man by Azazel are not knowledge from God, but instead from the fallen Nephilim, so Christians must avoid being enticed by them. That is why it is written, "Do not love the world or the things in the world. If anyone loves the world, the love of the Father is not in him" (1 John 2:15).

"Impiety increased; fornication multiplied; and they transgressed and corrupted all their ways. Amazarak taught all the sorcerers, and dividers of roots: Armers taught the solution of sorcery; Barkayal taught the observers of the stars; Akibeel taught signs; Tamiel taught astronomy; And Asaradel taught the motion of the moon. And men, being destroyed, cried out; and their voice reached to heaven" (1 Enoch 8:2–9). In these accounts and many others, it is clear that man received quite a lot of knowledge from spirit beings other than God himself. So we can conclude that when God asked man, "Who told you that you were naked?" (Genesis 3:11), the *who* refers to Satan and his fallen Nephilim. Knowledge has to be taught by someone, and Satan used that opportunity to instill his wicked, poisonous teaching in the mind of man.

Later Satan used other spirit beings to continue to teach man in ways that are against God's will, in his ongoing effort to destroy humankind as a whole. Satan was the first to instill corrupt knowledge in the heart of man. The Greek god Apollo is associated with knowledge, intellect, light, and the sun. Thus it is no coincidence that the first man-made objects to reach the moon were named after the god of knowledge: the Soviet Union's Luna [light] 2 mission in 1959 and Apollo 11 from the United States in 1969.

Some of man's knowledge is from God and other knowledge is from other spirit beings, but all knowledge is *of* God, who is omniscient. Knowledge can be used for both good and evil, but any knowledge not from God is demonic in nature. Why? Because it contains the venomous poison to ultimately destroy humankind, despite any good for which it might be employed in the meantime. Paul said, "We destroy arguments and every lofty opinion raised against the knowledge of God, and take every thought captive [evil knowledge] to obey Christ" (2 Corinthians 10:5).

Knowledge apart from God will appear to make sense to the unknowing, as though it's the right thing at the right time, thus raising false hope about the future. Yet any knowledge accepted by undiscerning man has always been twisted and incomplete. As Satan said to the woman regarding the tree in the garden of Eden, "For God knows that when you eat of it your eyes will be opened, and you will be like God, knowing good and evil." The goal is for twisted knowledge to lift up man to claim deity for himself; the more man's twisted knowledge increases, the more he believes that he is a god.

Knowledge has drastically increased in recent times. Buckminster Fuller, who created the knowledge doubling curve, wrote "that until 1900 human knowledge doubled approximately every century. By the end of World War II knowledge was doubling every 25 years. Today things are not as simple as different types of knowledge have different rates of growth. For example, nanotechnology knowledge is doubling every two years and clinical knowledge every 18 months. But on average human knowledge is doubling every 13 months. According to IBM, the build out of the 'internet of things' will lead to the doubling of knowledge every 12 hours."

What does this mean to us? An increase of knowledge is a sign that man has become more determined to be as God, since knowledge is the vehicle to make that happen. Knowing who provides the knowledge was paramount for Adam and Eve, and not all of man's knowledge was taught to him by God. Could it be that the rapid growth in knowledge today is being driven, yet again, by Satan and other spirit beings? He did it once in the garden of Eden, so he can do it again today. "For as were the days of Noah, so will be the coming of the son of man" (Matthew 24:37). How were things in the days of Noah? The Nephilim (fallen angels) were on earth passing all sorts of knowledge to man and committing abominations with man before God. But today, people who are wise and spiritual know that an increase in man's knowledge from any source other than God is twisted knowledge and will never be the whole truth.

Man's fascination with the heavens is important and should be investigated. Why are billions of dollars being spent on space exploration? Why are we looking for life on other planets? Why do we place satellites in orbit around Earth to record sounds and movements in the heavens? Is it just human curiosity or does man have a deeper purpose? I believe these things are done with a purpose. You've probably heard about government conspiracy, but what about angelic conspiracy? There are many important things for us to focus on, but we are so bombarded with media lies that it shifts our focus from the most important to the least important. The biblical story of the tower of Babel is remarkably similar to what we have today in the world of space exploration and NASA.

The Tower of Babel

The Tower of Babel was built by the Babylonians so they could reach heaven. That man wanted to go to heaven his own way is not a new idea; he has done this throughout history. Genesis 11 tells us about man's efforts to reach heaven to make a name for himself and avoid being scattered over the face of the earth. But within the pages of noncanonical, extra-biblical texts endorsed by Bible scholars, we find other reasons why man wanted to reach heaven. This is one reason why we believe that man is yet again playing a dangerous game by aiming toward the heavens. Let's delve into an account from Jasher 9:24–26 and see how it applies to us today:

And they began to make bricks and burn fires to build the city and the tower that they had imagined to complete. And the building of the tower was unto them a transgression and a sin, and they began to build it, and whilst they were building against the Lord God of heaven, they imagined in their hearts to war against him and to ascend into heaven. And all these people and all the families divided themselves in three parts; the first said, "We will ascend into heaven and fight against him"; the second said, "We will ascend to heaven and place our own gods there and serve them"; and the third part said, "We will ascend to heaven and smite him with bows and spears"; and God knew all their works and all their evil thoughts, and he saw the city and the tower which they were building.

Recently I was not surprised that man wants to build another military branch in the heavens, though I wonder whether the truth about its purpose is being told.

Today the purpose for ascending into the heavens, with NASA and Space X leading the way, is no different from the purpose for the Tower of Babel. Looking for another habitable planet is like trying to avoid God's coming judgment—or even trying to fight with God himself. We know that man cannot literally fight with our omnipotent God, but man can always try to counterfeit God's works to prove his nonexistence. Anyone who tries to prove that God does not exist, whether through science or some other means, is fighting with God.

Anthony Levandowski, one of the great minds in today's technology evolution, recently said this regarding knowledge and artificial intelligence: "Humans are in charge of the planet because we are smarter than other animals and are able to build tools and apply rules. ... In the future, if something is much, much smarter, there's going to be a transition as to who is actually in charge." Levandowski is raising a fair concern about man's acquired knowledge and ability to invent things over which we have no control. As much as we benefit from man's knowledge and intelligence, it can be detrimental if not used to glorify God. Levandowski continues, "What we want is a peaceful, and serene transition of control of the planet from human to whatever. And to ensure that the 'whatever' knows who helped it get along ... The 'whatever' [man-made invention/god] will hear everything, see everything, and be everywhere at all times." He thinks it will happen sooner than people expect, "not next week or next year; everyone can relax. But it's going to happen before we go to Mars." Man's increase in knowledge to reach the heavens has definitely placed him at odds with God, and more so when his knowledge is used not to glorify God but rather to disprove him or fight against him.

Building spacecraft to reach the heavens is no different from building a tower to reach into the heavens. Any object built with the purpose of ascending into the heavens is symbolically a tower, and its builders must eventually expect God's agent of confusion (babel) to fall upon them. Man is more knowledgeable now, and the methodology for ascending to heaven is now different, but man's objective—to make a name for himself and be his own god—has not changed. Could NASA's purpose in exploring the heavens be to make a name for themselves and claim that man is his own deity? In *Strong's Exhaustive Concordance of the Bible*, the Hebrew word *nasa* (#5377) means to deceive, beguile, seize, or utterly forget. No one knows for sure what man's exploration of the heavens is really about, but wasn't the serpent's purpose in the garden of Eden to *deceive*?

What is the danger? The closer man comes in his endeavor to reach that goal, the faster God will react to stop his action through confusion and judgment. Genesis 11:6–7 says, "And the Lord said, 'Behold, they are one people, and they have all one language, and this is only the beginning of what they will do. And nothing that they propose to do will now be impossible for them. Come, let us go down and there confuse their language, so that they may not understand one another's speech.'" The second biggest shift in the history of man, after the fall, happened when humankind was of one accord and pursuing the goal of reaching the heavens, because that is how all the different nations came to be. Could a third major shift happen before man is ready to go to Mars?

This time, the potential game changer is not speech confusion, but a man-made god. Could the "whatever" that man is creating, tampering with, or discovering actually be rooted in the power and knowledge of Satan? Apostle Paul said, "The coming of the lawless one is by the activity of Satan with all power and false signs and wonders" (2 Thessalonians 2:9). These are perilous times, my friends. Man's goal is to eliminate God and create his own god. Whatever man discovers or creates through technology and science could be the axis upon which our lives on this planet will pivot and change forever. This knowledge is another hiding place for death that, coupled with religion, keeps man from understanding his true spiritual potential.

What Is Man Really Looking For?

In analyzing man's quest for a hiding place, so far we have come up with two main places, religion and knowledge. Within these findings, we've explored the other source of man's knowledge outside of God and man's religious practices with futuristic intent. In both cases, we've found that man's practices are dangerous and assisted by Satan as part of his final blow to humankind. In the case of religion, man has created many diabolical cults and mystical places to promote and deify himself, while also deceiving many other people.

What is man really looking for? Let's go back to the Genesis account to decide if there's anything else to consider there. This will give us a commonsense approach to analyzing what could be either reality or a strong possibility, but not merely an opinion or speculation. After man's fall, we saw that God investigated and then sentenced each party according to his involvement (Genesis 3:14–21). If you are a serious student of the Word, you want to know more, because the story didn't end there. What happened next was truly eye opening.

Genesis 3:22 says, "Then the Lord God said, 'Behold, the man has become like one of us in knowing good and evil. Now, lest he reach out his hand and take also of the tree of life and eat, and live forever—'" This verse is the key to unlocking all of man's research and explorations. In this verse, God seems concerned about man's possible next step. When God says, "Behold, the man has become like one of us," he acknowledges that man has taken a step toward becoming as he is, but in what sense? Man now has knowledge of good and evil, which apparently had been secret knowledge reserved for God and possibly other divine beings. Man's violation of God's word, however, opens the floodgates so that other deities within the counsel of God can come and teach that knowledge to man. Now we can all admit, as God himself acknowledges, that knowledge could turn man into a god.

When we look at what man is able to do in every aspect of life today, there is no reason not to see him as a god, though not in the divine sense. In the medical field alone, man's knowledge has exploded as if he were his own creator. Man can now clone human or animal organs and body parts to save lives, and man's vast knowledge renders him as a god over certain diseases. This was also part of Satan's truth when he told Eve, "You will be like God, knowing good and evil" (Genesis 3:5b). There are many other examples that prove that man's knowledge has definitely turned him into a god, for the sake of discussion.

Genesis 3:22b reveals something interesting: "Now, lest he reach out his hand and take also of the tree of life and eat, and live forever—" Man worried God when he first disobeyed by eating of the tree of knowledge of good and evil, but even more troubling was the possibility of man committing a second action that could enable him to live forever. Why did God quickly expel man from the garden of Eden to prevent him from eating from the tree of life? Did man even know there *was* a tree of life in the garden? Why did God place angels with flaming swords to keep man away from the tree of life?

Before we delve into these questions, we can identify two characteristics of gods. First, a god has knowledge of good and evil, and second, a god is able to live forever. Man had obtained the knowledge of good and evil, but God prevented him from being able to live forever. Ever since then, man has been looking for a way back to the tree of life that God prevented him from reaching.

Why did God quickly expel man from the garden? If God hadn't prevented man from getting access to the tree of life, man would definitely have eaten from that tree, knowing that he would then be able to reach his goal of becoming a god and living forever. Can you imagine a sinful, disobedient man living in his sinful nature forever? What a catastrophe! But God, the master planner, had a plan of restoration in mind for man. Can we see the patience of God in the midst of all these chaotic situations? Yes, indeed, we *can* see it. What a wonderful God we serve!

Did man know there was a tree of life in the garden? It would be foolish to think that man did *not* know about it. The tree of life was at man's disposal, and he could have eaten from it with no punishment, because God had not commanded him *not* to eat from it. The tree of life was free to man. Do you get it? Yes, *free* of *law*. What man is now searching for was free and accessible to him in the garden of Eden. When he placed man in the garden, "the Lord God commanded the man, saying, 'You may surely eat of every tree of the garden, but of the tree of the knowledge of good and evil you shall not eat'" (Genesis 2:16–17a). I believe God was testing man by eliminating his access to the tree of the knowledge of good and evil instead of the tree of life. If God had forbidden man from eating fruit from the tree of life, man would have been curious about doing that as well. It's like telling a child to do the opposite of what you actually want him to do. Satan will always try to deceive man into doing the things that God has commanded him not to do, but not the things that God has not forbidden to him.

In chapters 27 and 28 of the *Apocalypse of Moses,* we find an interesting account of man after the fall. Let's pick up the story after God ordered the angels to cast man out of the garden:

> Thus he spake and bade the angels have us cast out of paradise: and as we were being driven out amid our loud lamentations, your father Adam besought the angels and said: "Leave me a little (space) that I may entreat the Lord that he have compassion on me and pity me, for I only have sinned." And they left off driving him and Adam cried aloud and wept saying: "Pardon me, O Lord, my deed." Then the Lord saith to the angels, "Why have ye ceased from driving Adam from paradise? Why do ye not cast him out? Is it I who have done wrong? Or is my judgment badly judged?" Then the angels

fell down on the ground and worshipped the Lord saying, "Thou art just, O Lord, and thou judgest righteous judgment."

But the Lord turned to Adam and said: "I will not suffer thee henceforward to be in paradise." And Adam answered and said, "Grant me, O Lord, of the Tree of Life that I may eat of it, before I be cast out." Then the Lord spake to Adam, "Thou shalt not take of it now, for I have commanded the cherubim with the flaming sword that turneth (every way) to guard it from thee that thou taste not of it; but thou hast the war which the adversary hath put into thee, yet when thou art gone out of paradise, if thou shouldst keep thyself from all evil, as one about to die, when again the Resurrection hath come to pass, I will raise thee up and then there shall be given to thee the Tree of Life.

For how long did God have that cherubim guard the tree of life? For as long as man is living, and until the resurrection day. Think about it. What could possibly be behind man's interest in knowing all that?

Before I continue, I would like to bring a little light to the pseudepigraphical writings. In Greek, *pseude* means "false" and *epigraphe* means "inscription." These are falsely attributed texts whose claimed authorship is unfounded, works whose real authors attributed them to past writers. Mark Kiley wrote that, in antiquity, pseudepigraphy was "an accepted and honored custom practiced by students/admirers of a revered figure." Just as a parent today would be proud to give his child the name of a revered athlete, an author in antiquity was honored to ascribe the name of a revered figure to his work. In biblical studies, the Pseudepigrapha are Jewish works written between 200 BC and AD 200, not all of which are actually pseudepigraphical. These works purport to be written either by noted authorities in the Old Testament or by people involved in Jewish or Christian religious study or history. "These works can also be written about Biblical matters, often in such a way that they appear to be as authoritative as works which have been in the many versions of the Judeo-Christian scriptures."

A word of caution: the Pseudepigrapha are not as authoritative as biblical scriptures, but they can help connect the dots in certain biblical stories where information is missing. This is the only reason why I use them here to support my investigation and narrative of man's biggest quest since the day he was cast out of the garden of Eden. This does not mean they are not accurate or valuable writings upon which conclusions can be based.

It's clear that man knew about the tree of life in the garden of Eden, so it wouldn't be strange for man to try to put his hands on it now. In fact, this is absolutely what man is after. We cannot deny that one of man's biggest quests since his expulsion from the garden of Eden has been to find his way *back* there to access the tree of life, which was forbidden to him.

Where was the tree of life in the garden? Genesis 2:9 says it was in the middle, so man would definitely have known about and been familiar with it. It might even have been next to the tree of knowledge of good and evil, and thus obviously known to man. The locations of these two trees is interesting, because they indicate that God was not hiding anything. Man had only to obey and trust God, and everything that he ever needed would have been given to him.

Why did God place angels with flaming swords to keep man away from the tree of life? God already knew about man's intention to access the garden and eat of the tree of life, so he created a security system that man cannot breach. On the other hand, knowing that the tree of life is guarded by mighty angels, man now seeks to communicate with spiritual beings beyond this planet to gain access to the forbidden gateway that leads to the tree of life. Man has to build a coalition to invade the garden of Eden and reach the tree of life that is being guarded and protected by God's angelic forces.

Man is spending trillions of dollars on space exploration and seeking communication with intelligent extraterrestrials. To acquire more knowledge, man is willing to go even to the sun. If man could find his way back, the increase of his knowledge would redefine our history in unprecedented ways. Alas, God has already told us the end from the beginning, that man's search will come out empty and void. Man will regain access to the tree of life only after the resurrection, for the tree of life was transported to the New Jerusalem city walls (Revelation 22:2).

God's Solution for Man's Quest

Knowing man's determination to access once again the tree of life to eat of it and live forever, God, in his compassion, draws up a plan to bring the tree of life to man, but in disguise. He wants to see if man, with all his acquired knowledge, will recognize the very thing for which he is looking. "For the wisdom of this world is folly with God. For it is written, 'He catches the wise in their craftiness'" (1 Corinthians 3:19). Man cannot see and understand. He is still wandering everywhere upon the face of the earth and now in the heavens. Can he find the tree of life? He cannot discern and understand the things of God.

Jesus said, "This is the bread that came down from heaven, not like the bread the fathers ate, and died. Whoever feeds on this bread will live forever" (John 6:58). Man wants to go to the heavens to find either a secret place to hide from death or the tree of life to live forever. Man has determined to put an end to death and live forever, but again, alas, man does not understand. When Jesus said, "Whoever feeds on this bread will live forever," that hint should have ended man's pursuit of the tree of life.

We can draw some parallels between the bread of life and the tree of life. In Genesis 3:22, "Then the Lord God said, 'Behold, the man has become like one of us in knowing good and evil. Now, lest he reach out his hand and take also of the tree of life and eat, and live forever—'" Man can eat from both the tree of life and the bread of life, and both the tree of life and the bread of life can make man live forever. Could it be that the tree of life for which man is searching has come to him in the person of Christ? Yes, absolutely, as a little boy named Jesus who was born in a manger at Bethlehem.

Although Jesus is like the tree of life, he never called himself by that name because he wants man to figure it out. Jesus asked Peter, "Who do people say that the Son of Man is?" (Matthew 16:13). He called himself "the true vine" (John 15:1) and said that every branch that attaches to him will have everlasting life. (What is a vine? Why is he talking about a branch that attaches to him?) What more did he need to say? Man needs to open his eyes and understand.

Jesus said in John 14:6, "I am the way, and the truth, and the life. No one comes to the Father except through me." Did Jesus know man would be looking for a way? Then he is the way. Did he know man's vehicle through any other way would be a lie? Then he is the truth. Did he also know that life is what man would be looking for? Then he is the life. All his claims concerning man's quest are accurate; otherwise why would he have made that bold statement? To do so without knowing the ultimate mind-set, goal, and heart of man would have been premature. Jesus got to the core issue and bluntly said what he knew man had been after since being cast out of the garden of Eden. Everything falls into place as we come to understand better what Jesus meant when he said, "I am the way, the truth, and the life."

With everything that God could have offered to man, why did he choose to offer everlasting life? That had been his plan even before man was created, because he knew that's what man would need and seek. He didn't offer eternal life to the angels who sinned, because they were already eternal beings.

If man truly desires to live forever, there is hope for that in Jesus Christ. Only Jesus offers the eternal life that man needs and that no one else can offer. Some people have taken Jesus at his word by faith, rather than committing crimes of treason against the human race in their eagerness to make names for themselves. This is an indication of true wisdom in those who are humble and believe they need grace instead of fame. Jesus offers the everlasting life that man has been seeking for millennia.

People who accept Jesus's offer find the solution to the death dilemma, and they have different terminology. In John 11:11–14 we read, "He said to them, 'Our friend Lazarus has fallen asleep, but I go to awaken him.' The disciples said to Him, 'Lord, if he has fallen asleep, he will recover.' Now Jesus had spoken of his death, but they thought that he meant taking rest in sleep. Then Jesus told them plainly 'Lazarus has died.'" For those who love him and accept him as their savior, Jesus talks of sleep rather than death.

The apostle Paul in 1 Thessalonians 4:13–15 said, "But we do not want you to be uninformed, brothers, about those who are asleep, that you may not grieve as others do who have no hope. For since we believe that Jesus died and rose again, even so, through Jesus, God will bring with Him those who have fallen asleep. For this we declare to you by a word from the Lord, that we who are alive, who are left until the coming of the Lord, will not precede those who have fallen asleep." Again, the terminology for believers has changed.

People who believe in Jesus's bold statement "I am the way, the truth, and the life" find the blueprint for what man has always wanted, and they will no longer walk in the fear of death. But people who want to make a name for themselves will never have eternal life unless they accept Jesus as the only way to the tree of life. Any effort by man to access the tree of life by any means other than Jesus Christ is a waste of time, money, knowledge, and energy. No invention or extraterrestrial intelligence can lead man there, because it is forbidden and heavily guarded by mighty angels. My friends, there is indeed a secret place to hide from death—and that place is Jesus Christ.

"I give them eternal life, and they will never perish, and no one will snatch them out of my hand. My father, who has given them to me, is greater than all, and no one is able to snatch them out of the Father's hand" (John 10:28–29).

"Jesus said to her, 'I am the resurrection and the life. Whoever believes in me, though he die, yet shall he live, and everyone who lives and believes in me shall never die. Do you believe this?'" (John 1:25–26).

In the Psalmist's Words

The Bible teaches us in the first verse of Psalm 91, "He who dwells in the shelter of the most High will abide in the shadow of the Almighty." There is a dwelling place in the shadow of Almighty God, a secret place where we can escape death, a place of protection and security. The psalmist continues in verses 2 and 3, "I will say to the LORD, my refuge and my fortress, my God in whom I trust. For he will deliver you from the snare of the fowler, and from the deadly pestilence." The psalmist understands that he is safe from deadly attacks by the enemy when he dwells in God's secret place. This shadow of the Almighty is actually Jesus Christ. Jesus is the shadow of the invisible God.

"He will cover you with his pinions, and under his wings you will find refuge; his faithfulness is a shield and buckler. You will not fear the terror of the night, nor the arrow that flies by day, nor the pestilence that stalks in darkness, nor the destruction that wastes at noonday. A thousand may fall at your side, ten thousand at your right hand, but it will not come near you" (Psalm 91:4–7). The protection that Jesus Christ offers to those who believe in him is indescribable. No armed forces or military might can assure such protection and security. You must take him by his word. This protection is not only physical, but even more so, spiritual. When we come to understand the battlefield of the spirit realm and the war that rages around those who believe in Jesus, we will see how important it is to take refuge under the wings of the Almighty.

> You will only look with your eyes and see the recompense of the wicked. Because you have made the Lord your dwelling place—the Most High, who is my refuge. No evil shall be allowed to befall you, no plague come near your tent. For he will command his angels concerning you, to guard you in all your way. On their hands they will bear you up, lest you strike your foot against a stone. You will tread on the lion and the adder; the young lion and the serpent you

will trample underfoot. Because he holds fast to me in love, I will deliver him; I will protect him, because he knows my name. When he calls to me, I will answer him; I will be with him in trouble; I will rescue him and honor him and show him my salvation. (Psalm 91:8–16)

If you are really looking for the secret place to hide from death, I can only offer the best one I know of, and that place is Jesus Christ, the son of the Almighty God. Accept him and he will protect you from the deadly attacks of the spirit of death and all others.

A Secret Place to Hide from Death

Have you ever wondered why people are dying? Can anything be done to stop death? Within the pages of this book, you will find the answers to those questions. This book will take you on a journey you have never taken before. You will come to understand why we die, explore the various unsuccessful efforts man has made to eradicate death, and, finally, discover the only place where we can avoid death. Those who are smarter have found it and been able to avoid death. Yes, you can hide and be protected from death.

References

Department of Health and Human Services. "US Annual Death Rate per 1,000 Population, 1900–2005." Vol. 54, no. 20 (August 21, 2007).

Harris, Mark. "Inside Artificial Intelligence's First Church of Artificial Intelligence." *Wired,* November 15, 2017. https://www.wired.com/story/anthony-levandowski-artificial-intelligence-religion/.

Kiley, Mark. *Colossians as Pseudepigraphy.* Biblical Seminar 4. Sheffield: JSOT, 1986.

"Mortality and Morbidity: Mortality in the 20th Century." *Visual News,* October 12, 2012. Abs. gov.au 4102.0 Australian Social Trends, 2001.

Schilling, David Russell. "Knowledge Doubling Every 12 Months, Soon to Be Every 12 Hours." *Industry Tap into News*, April 19, 2013. http://www.industrytap.com/knowledge-doubling-every-12-months-soon-to-be-every-12-hours/3950.

Shaver, Derek A. *Ultimate Apocrypha Collection: A Complete Collection of the Apocrypha, Pseudepigrapha and Deuterocanical Books of the Bible. Volume 1: Old Testament.* CreateSpace, 2007.

Starr, Benjamin. "Visualizing Major Cause of Death in the 20th Century." *Visual News,* May 20, 2015. http://www.visualnews.com/2013/03/19/visualizing-major-causes-of-death-in-the-20th-century/.

"World Death Rate." *CIA World Factbook.*